I CHALLENGE
YOU

Paul and Judith LeBlanc

WESTBOW
PRESS®
A DIVISION OF THOMAS NELSON
& ZONDERVAN

Scripture taken from the Amplified Bible, copyright © 1954, 1958, 1962, 1964, 1965, 1987 by The Lockman Foundation. Used by permission.

WestBow Press books may be ordered through booksellers or by contacting:

WestBow Press
A Division of Thomas Nelson & Zondervan
1663 Liberty Drive
Bloomington, IN 47403
www.westbowpress.com
1 (866) 928-1240

ISBN: 978-1-5127-8959-1 (sc)
ISBN: 978-1-5127-8960-7 (e)

Print information available on the last page.

WestBow Press rev. date: 06/16/2017

CONTENTS

INTRODUCTION

Paul and I wrote this book at a time in our lives when God was really pouring into us. He wanted us to tell everyone what lessons we had learned. Sometimes we learned these lessons the easy way, and sometimes we had to learn these lessons the harder way. Either way, we had learned these from the Holy Spirit and wanted to reach out to others who have in some way experienced trials and what we call "challenges." We call it challenges because in God's eyes, trials do not have to be looked at as negative. They can be a very positive experience as you overcome. We wanted to help others the way God had helped us in our times of need by sharing our very personal experiences and how God reached out to us in those times. We hope this books creates hope and childlike faith to our Father God, as you read our supernatural experiences, our wisdom we learned from the Father, and our faith and how we overcame through Jesus. We hope that what we learned can be very helpful to you as you face trials of every kind whether its overcoming a circumstance or its overcoming a thought pattern or a wrong belief, whether it's an emotion or it's a negative mind set. What we hope you get out of this book is more faith, in the One who is there for you in your circumstances and life journey, Jesus Christ. We hope you meet Him, who he is, in this book and that you are forever set on a new path of change. We pray that you will be open to the Holy Spirit as you listen and read the message that we have written from our hearts to yours. We pray that you would be receptive to His heart for yours in this book. We want you to know that God loves you just as you are. Take this book to a quiet place and let His love woo you into this book. Let his love change you as you just soak in this book. Let the words change you, as you just lay back and allow him to move in you and change you. And He will, don't worry. You don't have to do anything. Just be open and be ready for His glory to come and change you. We can never look back. Let this book take you into the newness of this season of your life. We believe that every person that has this book in their hands right now is because of the Lord's doing. He has wooed you from the time you were born and wants to change you right now in this season of your life. Let Him do that. There is a verse in the bible "search me and know me oh God." We pray this over the heart of your life. That you would be searched out by God and known by Him as you are. Don't wait until you have it all figured out. You just come with your little self and settle in His lap and read this book. He will do the rest. Because He loves you, and never will let you go. Just relax in Him and let Go!

From: The Authors of this book:

Judith and Paul LeBlanc

Before you read this book, I want you to know, that Jesus loves you so much, Just sit back and let him flow.

His eyes are on us as he watch and stare.

As a king upon a tree

No matter what happens he still cares

Day after day we ponder with worries

As Jesus focus on us He is never in a hurry!

Walking along the beach with foot prints in the sand

Blowing of the wind he takes our hands

Pain and sorrows He will take away

As he gets us ready for a new day

Our love is in the Lord we cannot deny

With peace and grace we soar to the sky

I challenge you to seek the Lord King Jesus

In every page.

Please give him your heart instead of having rage

If you delight in this poem that sounds so sweet

then give him your heart. He will make it complete.

I challenge you Book
Inspired by the Holy Spirit

Many waters cannot quench love, rivers cannot
wash it away. Song of Songs 8:7-8

MIND GAMES

Many waters cannot quench love, rivers cannot wash it away. Song of Songs 8:7-8

This verse was the verse God gave me at the beginning of the start of a wrestling match between darkness and light. I didn't know what I was getting myself into but I started just with a lot negative thoughts and emotions. I was just a babe in Christ, only been walking faithfully for a full year when I started to fear a lot of evil and would get a lot of scripture that I thought God was speaking to me, but it really was Satan trying to pretend to be God, so I would get confused and worried and scared. So I would self prophesy which is predicting something that is not true about your future.

I attended a church every Tuesday called Embassy Young Generations and was leading a dance team there. When I started going into a heavy depresson, I started to fear death and the enemy. I had to quit my dream of being a dance teacher for church all around the globe. I wasn't able to lead at the time because of all the emotions of my past floating around me and I started to worry, getting confused and not realizing who was talking, God or the enemy.

I remember my mentor telling me at the time, Judith you have to take your thoughts captive if you don't things are going to get a whole lot worse. Unfortunately I did not take the challenge at the time, believing I couldn't really do it, and allowing things to cycle out of control.

I CHALLENGE YOU

We are more than conquerers in Jesus Christ. Romans 8:37

We all can go learn from life circumstances, or save the negative from learning from someone else. I challenge you to do what my mentor who was inspired by the Holy Spirit, told me, to take my thoughts captive.

"Well, you don't understand, Its my emotions, not my thoughts"

Well I do not doubt that your emotions are taking a toll on you if your thoughts are negative. Take the time to write out the thoughts you are thinking without really knowing it. Look at your circumstance. My circumstances at the time was really pulling me down and I was constantly praying and crying while praying. Help keep the vicious cycle away.

The Vicious Cycle:

1) negative circumstance
2) Negative thought "this will never end."
3) Negative emotion Sadness
4) Which leads to, if nothing changes, despair. This can change to depression if nothing changes.

Can you catch something in this cycle that does not abide by the word of God? I can, none of it does. You can either live by your circumstance or by the Word of God. If you are living by circumstances you will always be ruled by your emotions, because your thoughts will change as your circumstances change. If you live by the word of God, which never changes, you may not change your circumstances but you can remain stable on the rock (Christ) by thinking the Word and not your own random thoughts. (taking thoughts captive to the Word of God) Taking every thought into captivity according to what the Word says, and then starting to experience joy, peace, etc instead of sadness because you are not being ruled by your circumstances, you are allowing God's word to be above the circumstance, allowing the word to change the emotions.

ASK AND YOU SHALL RECEIVE

When I was going through a lot of battling against the flesh with depression and anxiety, I started to get weary. I started thinking about my husband who I had not met yet and how having him by my side would help me get through this. I started praying from my heart for my husband to come, to pray with me and I never really knew how God would answer me so quickly. After a week of this, soon my husband Paul came into my life and started working with me to move towards God and God told me he was going to be my help mate.

Delight yourself In the Lord and He will give you the desires of your heart.
Ask and you shall receive, seek and you shall find, knock and the door will be open to you
I challenge you to ask for what you desire!
He wants to fulfill all of your desires

If you haven't received, maybe you have not asked
If you ask with the right motives and with faith in your Abba Father, you will receive!
Receiving brings you closer to God and allows you to experience the joy he died for you
     to have
Don't live in a poverty mentality when all you have to do is ask Him.

You may be saying in your mind and your heart, "But I don't know what to pray for"
Begin by starting out with thank you for what I already have
Then be honest with God, quiet yourself and see what your heart has been telling you that you need or desperately desire. Then be bold and ask! If you do not receive as quickly as I did, do not get discouraged, just keep asking.

One of the steps I did to receive my blessing, which is my husband, is that I delighted myself in the Lord.

He tells us in the word to delight ourselves in the Lord and he WILL give us the desires of our hearts. As I was watching and waiting for my husband, I was reading the word, worshiping God and spending time with Him. I wasn't waiting and complaining to God every time I had a chance. I was still spending quality time with Him, delighting myself in his company. In return, he brought my husband to me, and soon after, we started dating.

BONE OF MY BONES, AND FLESH OF MY FLESH.

Paul.

When Paul came into my life, I was worn out on religion, stressed to the max, and battling spiritual darkness that was far beyond myself. God was telling me things about my future that was to come expecially when it came to my future relationship with my husband. Before I met Paul, I had been beaten down by Satan and was desperately seeking God trying to find refuge and safety. I would look for it in the church, but a lot of times they didn't have the resources and even safety I was needing at the time. I needed someone who was walking very close to God, who knew how to pray and knew a lot about spiritual war fare. I needed protection because I was being brutally attacked.

When I met Paul, I was sitting across from him at a restaurant after one of the young adults group night at our church called the Embassy. He boldly came up to a quiet and worn out me, and shook my hand saying "you are a woman of God!" I thought he was very interesting and bold, and he sat down starting to speak into my life, God using him to minister to me. I soon learned he walked in the office of a prophet, which means he would speak into peoples lives, based on what God was wanting to tell them and he would deliver the message, either of encouragement, or correction. He also owned his own record label called Faith Records. I was at the time very interested in getting my music out, and looking for someone to record demos of my music so we kept in contact. I did not know it then but the Holy spirit was also leading him to me, and he was very drawn to me as well.

We began to talk on the phone and go out in his car to read the word and praise God and speak in tongues against powers and principalities that were coming against me at the time. I was going through a lot of healing from my past so the enemy was trying to hold me down and wouldn't let me go without a fight. Paul was being led by the spirit and so he came faithfully to my home every day after work and take me out to pray with me. I thought he was a really caring person but I never thought anything more until one day while we were out listening to God speak, I heard God tell me that this man I was sitting beside was my help mate. I looked at Paul and I again heard the same word drop into my spirit with a real peace from heaven. That same night Paul also gave me his number of his home phone. We started calling eachother more often after that. We would talk about Jesus and he would teach me how to simplify God.

I had become so analitic in my faith and I had lost the joy of my salvation. Paul helped me discover this again. We fasted together and fought against spiritual forces, and we soon began to form a deep level friendship. Soon after we became involved on a deeper level and would go out for dates as well. He shared a few visions to me that he saw of us together, the visions were so deep and beautiful and they sounded just like me and what I would do. He started to tell me that he asked God if he could marry me and God said Yes, all you had to do was ask my son. I was so shocked that God answered my prayers!

As our relationship deepened in the love of Jesus, we grew as friends and we grew inlove. I had to confront a big fear of mine though. I was afraid that I was going to loose him. I was afraid of love. I was afraid to love and be loved. I knew that paul was my other half, bone of my bone and flesh of my flesh, and that God was challenging me not to run but to stick close to this man and to Jesus. Also I know that if I denied this man, that I would be denying Jesus as I could tell Jesus was in this man and I also felt that this man was so deep in my heart as if eternity had sketched him there all along. When we spent time together every day felt like the last one. I was going through a lot of turmoil but it didn't scare him away. I saw him faithfully come to me every day. I felt like I was suffering and in turmoil. Every night I would cry out to God for repentance feeling bad that I couldn't love Paul more than I was. I felt so afraid of loving him but I didn't want to walk away. I needed our relationship but God kept on speaking words to us to stay together. We both knew it was for more than just fun, that it was for a bigger purpose that both of us had to complete before our time on earth was up.

But eventually I couldn't hold on any longer with the turmoil going on and I was sent to the hospital to get better. Paul stuck by me through it all and showed me Jesus undying love and commitment to me. I knew Jesus was not giving up on me. Infact I felt him closer than before throughout all this process. He was my ever present help in times of my troubles. I wanted to give up but then as soon as I thought that, I would hear that there is only one Judith and we don't realize that as believers in Jesus how much we affect the world around us. As I was there, I started to get stronger. I prayed and would sing to Jesus and I started to fight back against these spiritual forces. During this time, I learned an important way of how God can work in your life. Sometimes we want things instantly, but sometimes God just wants to walk with you through it, and instead of getting rid of the pain and worries right away, he works with you to build you up and make you stronger, by a day to day process. I also learned to rest in Jesus Christ, and that is when God can work most in your life. I didn't have to understand everything that God was doing I just needed to rest in Jesus like a little baby would rest in their mothers arms. Things started looking better for me and I decided I was not going to let what doctors reports about me said, to define me, and my health and in all, my life. And one more great thing: my husband was here for me for life. I had another reason to fight back, because I had an amazing future to look forward to and someone who loved me for who I was, and was waiting in faith and patience for my miraculous recovery.

I challenge you in all this: to find the positive blessings in your life and never give up
Philipians 4:8

What ever is true, what ever is noble, what ever is right, what ever is pure, what ever is lovely, what ever is admirable, if anything is excellent or praiseworthy, think about such things.

With prayer and petition, I started casting my cares on God and letting his presence fill all my senses with joy and peace. I let him change the way I thought. At first this was very challenging but as I kept worshiping him and letting my cares out and being positive in my thoughts and words, I started to change my attitudes and mind. Instead of looking where i wasn't, I started looking forward day by day. I looked to Jesus, not where I was at in my circumstances. He would always talk to me through a person or through the day to my heart, saying to just rest. I had to relearn how to live. I learned a peace that is supernatural, that comes through prayer and worshiping God.

I was very much a worrier in the beginning but God brought a verse into my life that has stuck with me throughout "be anxious for nothing but by prayer and petition, with thanksgiving present your requests to God and the God of peace will guard your hearts and minds in Christ Jesus. Philipians 4:6

I felt overwhelmed with life at times, but when God's love got a hold of me, the love became a stronghold that broke every anxiety and worry. Another tool that helped break off anxiety and depression was when I started to read the bible and God would show me promises for myself that I could rely on. I challenge you to let the word decrease your worry and fears. Let words transform you, they are not just any words, they are the very words from the breath of God, they are alive and they can change you. I thought it would take something more complicated to transform my thinking but all you have to do is replace the old with the new. I read his word and welcomed him to read with me and when I was finished I was in a much positive attitude and full of faith. The Word of God does change people. There is nothing too big for God – nothing is impossible with God. Hebrews 4:12.

THE FATHERS LOVE AND
FAITH LIKE A CHILD

One day I was laying in my bed, just soaking in the Lord's music. Soaking is to just lay there and allow the music to bring you closer to Jesus's heart. As I was laying there, desperate to know him more, I was shown a picture form the Lord in my heart and mind. It was a picture of a little girls feet. Jesus was washing her feet between her toes. I knew immediately as it flashed before me that this little girl was me and those were my little feet. My eyes were on the Lord and he took me to a place of deep worship where he showed me the fathers love for me. He loves me and wanted to demonstrate that love by just being with me to wash my feet. I had been through a lot of suffering at the time and was going through a trial and needed to see the Fathers love for me. How I was just a little girl in the eyes of a big Father and he was just washing my feet delighting in my little feet who he created for himself. He was tenderly washing me, and soaking me in this water. I needed to see this to know how the Father wants to be with me. He delights in his creation and wants us to be just as deeply delighted in Him as our father. Demonstrationg the love of God is deeply communicated through out worship. Laying down ones life for another is a place of deep intimacy God wants to take us to as our Father. If anyone has not been through a good relationship with their father, know that you can experience the Fathers love through Jesus Christ. He demonstrated His love for us when he died upon the Cross and became like us so that he would bring us back to the Father, who delights in us. He loves us so much and doesn't see us the way we see ourselves. In fact he wants us to climb apon his lap so that we can be told who we truly are by spending time with Him. He brings us up highter when we come to him and lay down all our concerns and give him our time and our love. Enjoyment and pleasure is one of the greatest things the Lord, our Father created. He created this so that He could enjoy and find pleasure in the ones he created and so they could come to find pleasure and enjoyment in the Father. So many times I have seen people who are worn out on religion and weary from the battles they have faced. They come to the Father and just collapse in his arms, too tired to carry themselves anymore. And that was not the way God created us to function. He wants us to have a sound mind and peace, but instead we are weighed down by anxious thoughts weary burdens and we forget why we were even created. So many people I have seen have sold themselves to others, in an attempt for temporary security and a sense of identity but I have learned, that no one owns me. There is only One who owns me, and that is Jesus Christ and God the Father and the Holy spirit, all in One. He desires to know me. He is the One who deserves my life, because he is the only one who laid down his life and paid the price for it. To forget that and go on with my life without him, is like forgetting the one who really died for me, because I chose to reject him. God will not make you choose him, he wants you to choose him out of love, not out of fear. You can trust Him to own your life when he paid such a big price for it. He died his blood poured out, naked and nailed to the cross for all to see. He paid a huge price, so he would never treat you poorly, and never lead you astray. You can know that he has the best interest for you. He would only take really good care of you and be a great friend to you, if you would just let him into your heart and your life.

Being a child of God is really easy. Its not a job, its not worldy understandin. Being a child of God has to be revealed by the Holy spirit to you and you would know you are a child of God be cause He would reveal it to your heart. Being a child of God means you get to climb apon the lap of the creator of the universe and he will tell you secrets to your heart and you would be free in His presence. He brings you closer to your heart through being with Him. Its not a striving thing. One of the things I had to learn and I believe is a learning curve for a lot of beleivers is that we feel deep down in our core that we are not good enough, or worthy enough for Jesus. So we strive and strive to earn His grace, his unmerited favor. His love and acceptance for us. So much that we grow tired and faint, and we turn back or give up. But God is calling us into a new place. He is saying much more these days to His beautiful bride. He is calling us to come home, to a higher place than we have ever been or seen or imagined. He has planned before creation of this intimacy of love and of grace, this quiet place of understanding between Him and His creation. Its yearning even the creation itself, is yearning for this quiet place. To be redeemed back to the place and time when God created Eden and adam for Himself. It was a quiet trusing place where only God and Adam could be. Eventually Eve came in and there was a deep fellowship between the three of them. But it was not a place of striving. It was a place of deep deep rest. But as we know, they sinned and broke communion and perfect fellowship with God. He loved them so much that as they realized they were naked and ashamed and hid from God, he clothed them. God knew that some day he would bring htem back to this place of deep intimacy through his Son, the perfect One, the Perfect atonement and that at this age in time, he would recreate this reaction between the Father and the people and would bring them back to the Father who knows them.

But I hear the Lord telling me this to His people : My people don't know why I died for them. They have heard all the wrong answers from man. When I createrd them, it was out of my passion and love and out of my goodness that I just wanted to be blessed and make a blessing. I am a worshiper at Heart and I wanted to give out of the abundance of worship in my heart. I bless. It was me who wanted to be blessed. Its what a Father does. I don't want a people who will be controlled by what man says, I want a people who are fully inlove with My heart, and my desires, and my will for their lives. I want a laid down lover in spirit and in truth, in speech and in action. You are my bride, and you are my children. I made you and that is why I can trust you. I believe in you, do you believe in me? My bride? My dove? I am a faithful watcher of your hearts, and I will come to you. I am your husband, not on earth but in heaven, and I will always be husband to you. You have my seed in you. When I made you I had a plan. A beautiful plan. But I must get this message across, I made man for myself. I didn't make you for someone else. Noone else can create you like I did. Noone else can tell you who you are.

Before I go on, I want to share something about the Father. His heart is close to children. He loves little children of the world. And he says let the little children come to me for theirs is the kingdom of Heaven. He delights in us as little children. And he looks at us with joy before to him we are his children, who don't know a lot yet but are learning as he guides us hand in hand. So we don't need to beat ourselves up, or tear ourselves down when ever we mess up. He wants us to love ourselves the way he loves us. He wants us to take pride in who we are because our Father created us. And unless we come as little children to Jesus, we will never be able to enter the kingdom. He wants to laugh with us and let go with us, letting that burden go, that negativity, that the world can rub off on you and renew your youth in His presence. He birthed us and he desires us to go through life with him, come to him for everything and bring everything to Him. He deeply hurts for us when we are hurt and he deeply cares for us like no one could ever care. So han on, anyone who is in deep waters, right now, because God the Father wants to share with you His mercy and love. He wants to assure you its not the end of the world. Sometimes things are tough but when you just rest in the rest of God, you learn that its just a season and that you are being guided by Love. By Jesus Himself. He never lets yhou go. And he never lets you gie. He never gives up on you, even when you want to give up on yourself. So hang on there.

Beleiving in Jesus is a child like thing. You have to just trust that He is there, hanging onto your hand and that you are safe in His arms. If you don't have this child like faith yet, let it enter you. You canot go wrong, you have nothing to loose but to empty yourself on Him and He will take you as you are. It might not feel nice at the time but He knows you. You have to trust Him that He can wipe your tears away and bring you out of that pit. He can do anything if you believe like a child would believe in her Daddy or his Daddy. He neev r said you would have to be perfect to be in His grace. All you have to do is be. He designed you to Be. Come as you are and he will show you the love you have always wanted. He knows what you need and he knows you need to be loved and held. This world can get rouch like rough tides crashing on the shores but He is calling us home. He says "take up your cross my beloved and come to me. I know you by name and you are mine. In time you will forgive yourself, you will believe again and you will have a new heart. You don't have to try with God.

Jesus is our life
In seeking his glorious ways and staying from all kinds of strife.
The power we have in him .
Keeps us from greater sin .
He died for you and I
We show our love then sigh.
It's the gift that really counts .

He is more to you than you could ever amount.
There is happiness in a lot of ways to come .
Just believe in him and know where you came from.
Holy spirit of truth will guide us in the right path
To give us courage and strength that will last.
A lot of people don't have to stress .
Why bother bringing your self to that mess .
Can you see your self walking in disguise
There is no one like jesus who will compromise
Just give Him your heart today, and you will not be swayed.
The End.

LISTENING TO GOD AND NOT YOURSELF.

I wanted to discuss about different challenges in my lifestyle and the principles of how to lean on Jesus and not on man or worldly views which I really struggled with as growing up in a Christian environment in which my parents taught me very good wisdom, but being the way I was, I rebelled and did not listen until I got hurt.

My parents were very good at disciplining all four kids and taught us right from wrong and encourage us with the word of God and regular principle of everyday life sometimes looking back I wish I listened it was for my own good .When we have these struggles we need to bring this to Jesus for he will undo your circumstances in not listening or just being rebellious. This rebellion had followed me quite a long time until I brought the problem to the Father, and eventually I got delivered. As time passed this came back 7 times stronger because I didn't follow the advice of Jesus which got me no where.

Did you know this fact, that when you do not take heed, or (listen) we can end up in turmoil and its not always the enemy sometimes its our own doing we need to run to Jesus about this he can take away guilt and shame selfpity . We can really start listening to our self or we can get the advice of our heavenly father which one would you choose ! Because I would choose God ways, I challenge yourself to this circumstance this would be very helpful to you. Rebellion is a sin towards God coming from our actions. Just to go back to God and Lucifer (satan) the archangel did not listen to God's command or advice. For he wanted to be better than God and because of pride he fell from heaven. The meaning of rebellion and listening means that you as a character do things the opposite what your mind is thinking for example your parents begin tell you a certain phrase but you decide to things a different way . Refers to being controlling which leads to pride, haughty, jealousy. All these situations can be destroyed in your lifestyle by the blood of Jesus.

As the years went by I could remember growing up I slowly started listening and less rebelling this didn't happen overnight it took some time by getting help with Jesus volunteering to go to a lot of healing clinics as well as seminars which Jesus tore down a lot of baggage which I did not need in my life .

Just remembering a famous football player who played with Toronto Argonauts' his name was Brian Warren A fantastic person and man of God. Looking back when we spoke he was always checking my walk with Jesus and realizing he was caring for my salvation and was accountable to him that was amazing we lost contact . But he would of made an awesome mentor and Jesus stepped in and brought someone else it was like a chess game for Jesus had to recondition me in order to listen the voice of God and not falling into rebellion .

Listening to God voice verses Satan voice and demon's as we grow or come to know Jesus "for the first time we can ask Jesus to be our friend" also asking him to start hearing God voice this might take some time which involves in a lot praying and spiritual which speaking in unknown language to Jesus this is called tongues of fire from the holy spirit having the intimacy with Jesus Christ . Lets talk about hearing From God my experience with listening was kind of difficult this might be easy for some and for others depending what Jesus wants for you .Remember it not on our time frame but this is on the Love of our father's perfect timing which he will speak to us even through a donkey here is some scriptures to help you study, Jeremiah 43:7 they did not hear the voice God (quoted from scripture) also Exodus 15:26, Acts 7:31 these circumstances helped myself to understand his voice let me explain when you begin to hear unknown speech words like you can take your friends car without he or she permission or the saying the nice guys finish last, that is a lie from the enemy who tries to make yourself to listen and believe in the unfailing truth. Also Satan can seriously trick us listening to negative word that don't line up with God word. You will begin to notice the difference between the two but if we pray a lot more we receive much power from God and able to hear Jesus speak these situation come from having a clear conscience, clean heart and a stable mind this allows us to move in the present of the most high God as he cleanse your mind hearing that uttering voice of God .I challenge you to read the scriptures and pray because Jesus waiting for you at the door as he calls us to follow him and I sure you with in his grace of timing we will hear his voice clear as bell this will come to pass in Jesus name .

Listening is a big part of our life style this very important so that you will be able to walk in the father's agape love and not doing the old ways of life having that new beginning by listening to his truth,direction, because hearing his voice can allow you to hear signs, warnings,prophesy, encouragement and many others . Please let Jesus speak into your life there is so much joy and peace to discover because my beautiful wife is starting to listen to God voice remember we can prosper and do any circumstances through our personal savior King Jesus Shalom.

INTIMACY AND TRUST

"He who dwells in the shelter of the Most High will abide under the shadow of the Almighty. Psalms 91

God is calling us to come closer to Him. To know Him in the most intimate way. He calls us first by name, and we respond. As we come running towards Him, He will never back away. He runs first to us and we respond by running towards Him. In Simple trust, we abide in Him. By believing in His grace and perfect love we will never fail. Our hearts rise like the dawn. As the Holy Ghost radiates on us. Blessed be the name of the Lord! His love never fails. In a moment, all our troubles can disappear as we dwell in Him. Beside Him, we can do anything, discover anything, and believe in anything He says. Because He knows us, we can be molded into the image of Christ who dwells in us. Believing can create a whole new world for us. Picture this, the God of the universe is madly inlove with you. He yields to you and asks you to come on the wildest adventure of a lifetime. As we begin to trust Him, He begins to grow in us a faith deeper than words, and a trust that can never be broken or hindered. Because in life, that is the number one thing we need. Faith and trust in a God who is never changing. Because then we can face any kind of evil or any kind of trial that we need to overcome. We can't do it alone, but we need a creator who can do it in us and through us. Because He knows us, we are to know Him. How can we trust someone we don't know? We trust Him because He died for us. We trust Him because He cannot do us wrong. No one will know you like God knows you. No one will believe in you like Jehovah Jireh, the provider of all your needs. When we begin to lean on Him for everything, He begins to move in you like never before. Because He loves you so much, He will never lead you astray. We need to begin to trust in the One who made us, for Himself, who loves us so much and takes us right where we are. We need to trust that. Only One can be so Kind. Only one can be so forgiving, so gentle, so inlove with you, a needy, sinful person who cannot save themselves. Only God can do that. We are so hopeless without Him. We are in need of His miracles in our lives, and it is only when we yield to Him and grow in Him that we are really allowing Him to create this new world for us, that is designed specifically for you. How you love, and how you yield to Him, that is the key to this intimacy, and growth in God.

Because you are reading this, I declare and believe that you are wanting this intimacy with God. God wants it with you too. He wants to be madly inlove with you and for you to be so madly inlove with Him too. He created the world for you, because He wanted to know you and for you to be known by Him. You are not by yourself, you are never alone. He wants you to know that you have been lied to by the enemy of your soul. He has fed you lies from the beginning, and they are not nice lies. Being told lies has distorted your view on who God is and who God has been and who God will always be. He has also told lies about you and who God wants you to be. But don't be fooled. He is not your friend, he is your adversary and he will not let go of you without a fight. But trust this, God is for you. A shield, a defender. If you are weak, seek the Lord. Believe that He wants to have you healed. Believe that he will defend you in your times of weakness. Believe that He will never let you go. If you are under attack, know that He loves you so much, and wait on Him. You will begin to trust Him as you dwell in the shadow of the Most High. He loves you so much, all you have to do is wait and trust Him. He will fight your battles. Just believe He can and that He loves you. Ask and you shall receive. Seek and you shall find. Knock and the door will be opened to you. Matthew 7:7. God wants you to begin to seek Him. Start by asking Him for what you need. Give your heart all to Him and He will give you all the blessings in the world. Go to Him in faith and trust, and tell him all that you need and he will give you rest. Matthew 11:28. Blessed are those that are hungry for they will be filled. Matthew 5. Remember that only God that created the universe will be really the one who will help you. No man can do this for you. Remember that the enemy of your soul, Satan, hates you and will try to use people to distort your image of who you are, and who God is and why you are here. Really watch out for those people because there is an enemy who really wants to destroy you. Take heart though, God is here and he is watching you. You are like a sparrow in his hand that will not fall to the earth apart from him knowing it first. Matthew 10:29.

The liar of your soul wants to tempt you. He wants to stop you from receiving anything and everything from the Father of our souls, God. He plants in us words of faith and the enemy wants to destroy all the work of God by planting words of doubt and guilt, shame and condemnation. Do not follow his voice. They are just lies planted there to get you to fall away from God and all that He created you to be. Listen to the Fathers voice, which is also planted in you to keep you with Him always. If you are asking for help from Jesus, then believe that he will help you. You need to be on the watch for the adversary. He seeks to kill steal and destroy. Blessed are those who are merciful. Your enemy is not human beings. Eph 6:12. We are here to bring the Kingdom of Light to the lost and the broken. We are not here to condemn but to help and heal those who need it. Trust in God, not in humans. But be merciful to those who deny Jesus, and to those who deny who you are too. Those who are against you and what you are created for by Your God are those that are also against God and what He has created in you. Be kind to one another, and get aggressive in the spirit against those principalities, not in the flesh. We were never created to go after the enemy alone, so know that there is a God who is greater than the one who is in this world. We are not the ones to come at him, but God in us is. We fight our battles in the spirit, where the enemy cannot see us or hear us or get to us. We are shielded and protected by our Author of our faith. But when we try to get into the fight in our flesh, we are stepping on the enemy's toes and provoking him. We cannot win this on our own, we are acting in faith when we speak in tongues, when we bless others when they persecute us and lie to us.

INTIMACY

"in quietness and trust"

Before you hit yourself over the head with this book because of all the challenges we are calling you to, trust me, I know. It can be feel overwhelming. But before you decide to do that, let us put a pause on all that challenges and sit and ponder for a bit. In other words, let us be still.

God does not expect you and I to do this on our own. He never did. In fact, that is why He tells us in the new testament from Jesus Himself, that He would be leaving but He would send each of us the Holy Spirit who would dwell in us and teach us in all things. He would be our leader and our advocate, or friend. So don't expect that we are perfect people or that you have to do this by yourself. He never once told us that we would be these perfect people with perfect lives. He knows we are limited in strength, wisdom and knowledge within yourself but in the Holy spirit, who is God, we can draw from His strength, His wisdom, and knowledge love peace and joy. His patience and His faith. He teaches us this through our will being transformed into His will by spending time in His presence. We can never know what we have with us unless we get to know Him, the Holy Spirit who is our helper. Otherwise, we are going through life not knowing who it is who really is with us.

People kind of blast through life, and wonder why they never got to know the One true God like they wanted to. We tend to want it all right now. All the resources, all the wisdom and knowledge, all the gifts from God. But this culture needs to slow down. The western culture needs to stop what they are doing, and start by being little babies who go back to the basics. We need to learn before we teach. We need to grow up but we cannot expect ourselves to know everything God knows, right now. We have to become like little children really, before we can increase in wisdom and strength. We need to know our creator before we figure out ourselves.

So rest, child, and let God begin to fill you with His love. What do babies need? They need rest, and lots of it. They need love and lots of it. Nutrition and lots of it. We get so caught up in the wisdom of this world and we forget that we really are not all that complicated, when it all comes down to it. We all need love, rest and nutrition to grow. If we cut that off and deprive us of that, we have a bunch of grumpy immature christians who are depriving themselves of the calling on their lives to know God, who is love and to be known by God. Being known by God is really something that takes time. My husband once was teaching me something about God's way versus our own way. I was going through a situation that I had never faced before.

My husband turned to me and said, you know God is not looking for perfection, He is looking for availability in a person. Knowing this lifted the burden of striving and I was able to start resting instead, turning my worries over to God knowing that as I became more available with him in my time, that I would grow in intimacy which is what I deeply desired. It takes time to grow though, so do not expect to get this right away. He is very patient with you and wants you to know Him because He knows that you cannot live without His presence. You can try but you will not know the amazing grace that comes from spending time in His presence. He knows that you can only hold so much in your little mind, your little body and your little heart before you go into overwhelming and burn out. Why don't we turn everything off once and a while and learn to crawl up on our Creators lap and allow Him to do what He wants to do for us? Give Him your time and He will do amazing things in your life. Allow Him to mold you and transform you into the beautiful person that you are. He will do the rest. If you allow His rest to free your mind and your heart from the world's burdens and sorrows. For God so loved the world that He gave His only Son, that who ever believes in Him shall not perish but have ever lasting life. –John 3:16. Meet Him half way, give Him your time, your energy, your heart and He will rest in you and cause His face to shine on you. He will finish the work He started in you as you rest in Him, you will overcome everything you may be facing. Well how do I rest, you may be thinking. Our culture has so much pushed us into doing and doing and doing that we have really needed to relearn how to just simply be. Resting is a deep down and knowning that Jesus has already finished the work. At the cross, when Jesus took our sins and died for us and then rose again 3 days later, He finished the work that needed to be done. When we look to the cross, we are already made whole in Him. Already healed, already perfect in Heaven where we are seated at the right hand of the Father in Jesus. So all our troubles fade away as we see Jesus, nailed there for our afflictions and has already taken the pain away. I know this may seem hard to understand but if you will just sit there and patiently wait for the Holy Spirit to see you through, you will understand this in time.

We all want the best for us now, but God sees the end from the beginning and He knows what is good for your overall wellbeing. We may not understand the difficulties at the time but as you cultivate a relationship with the Lord, we have understanding more in time, and also it will lessen the blows of the enemy in our lives, allowing us to live in victory and to trust Him more. We need to trust Him in this life, or else all falls apart. But when we get to know Him, we can begin to walk more in faith, and more freeing lifestyle because we are decreasing and He is increasing. We need not to be afraid or feel like a failure because Jesus has already paid the price for our lives. We are only beginning to see a glimpse of Him but in time we will know him as we are already known by Him. We need to learn to say "all is well with my soul." We have to be smart in our lives, how we live, how we walk, how we talk. We want to be jealous lovers of Jesus, where we don't watch the things that attract others because our desires have been molded to His desires. We don't worry like others because our thoughts have started to match up to our Father's word. We are able to trust because we trust ourselves to the Perfect One, who will never leave us. Wait upon Him and He will come to you. As you meet Him half way, you will see a huge difference in your life. God does not limit himself with us. We only limit ourselves. But if we walk towards Him we will see that He does want to help us, and will help us as we keep walking towards Him. Don't give up because one day you will see a huge difference, a huge breakthrough in your life from living every day in a place of abandonment with God, reaching for His hand and waiting for Him to come through for you. You must wait with a childlike faith. It builds and builds as you yield to the Master. Childlike faith is a knowing your Father will provide for you. It is not being negative but it is having a positive mindset like our Father in heaven that He is going to do amazing things and turn things around for you. You can trust Him. Because He is a good Father and knows what you want and need. Come to Him on your knees and He will lift you up. Where ever you are right now, if you are feeling a drawing of Him towards you to a deeper knowing of Him as your Father, and want to know Him in a deeper intimacy of trust, I challenge you to stop what you are doing and say this prayer with me. "Abba Father, I am longing for more of you. I know I am in need of your love and that I do not have enough of it in myself to love you, others or even myself. I am done striving and doing things my own way. Lord, I want to have a simple trust in you and a childlike faith. I run to you now Oh God, and pray that you will meet me here. In Jesus name, Amen.

I believe that there is a special anointing on this prayer for intimacy and that after you pray this you will know that your heavenly Father will come through for you. I don't know what you are going through, but I know that God so deeply wants you to turn to him in the midst of everything and learn to let go and let Him give you rest. He will listen to this prayer and you will begin to get up in the morning and be drawn to come and spend time with Him. Give Him your time, and it will grow into a deeper friendship as you stay faithful to that time with Him. And that is a friendship that no person can take from you.

God bless you my friends.

Poem lay your troubles down

Jesus has His perfect love to share .
just open your heart to let him care .
Don't live a life of hopelessness.
Search him in your saddest troubles .
Jesus will bring you out of your stumble.
His love is the way .
Which takes you to a better day.
Cast your cares upon his love .
For you are his lovely dove .
When all the chips come crashing down.
Jesus love will always be around .
Trying to find your place inside .
His love will grow far and wide.
You're the reason why he stares.

To take away all your fears.
Lay your troubles down today.
He will make the perfect way

By Paul LeBlanc

I challenge you.
Challenges for you to overcome.
We face many challenges in our every day life
And as we face these challenges
Some of the people will often give up.
In all circumstances, and some will keep trying until they succeed.
But when we have the power of the Glory of Jesus Christ in our lives,
Situations become much easier than we think.
In this last chapter, I want to challenge you to walk in a way of victory.

I found the secret in having a closer walk in Jesus Christ which is agape love, faith and honor. This is what God showed me along the years. He challenged me awhile back and it was not easy but as I persisted in this goal, God had to open my heart to understand the situation.

Have you ever faced different challenges?

Are you tired of having to go around in circles,well God can over come these situation by you leaving the problems at the throne of grace and Jesus will understand, so bring your troubles to Jesus, he is waiting give him a try . This can take a short time or long time depending on your attitude because Jesus is not a magician, sorcerer, he is the son of the Most high God and if you ask him he will open the doors but this will be on his perfect timing for your life .

Trust in Jesus for every circumstances and before you know it you are on your way to greater heights .

I really believe that anyone who comes to the father like a little child will be saved and nourished spiritually will become physically stable in he or she lifestyle just by the positive thinking like Jesus .

One day I met a sincere friend his name was Richard Silvera. We became like brothers. I have never felt so close to him. He would give the shirt off his back for me. That's like Jesus. A wonderful man. As years went by, he came to me and asked me to start up a gospel record company. I was in awe about this. This sat well with my spirit and there was very much peace. Before we knew it, this company started to take off like a rocket. Jesus was the master of this whole event and came to pass. We travelled to kingdom bound and met a lot of famous Christian bands and artists through this record company. We were just getting started. God opened up a lot of doors because it was His perfect timing. This situation was a perfect example of how to wait on Jesus Christ for everything because timing is of the essence.

If we decide to go on our own ideas and instincts, for example, if you meet the girl or guy you think you fell in love with, and you are just about to marry that person, some get cold feet and some get mixed feelings about the person who they are going to spend the rest of their lives together. So, we must go to God, for the right answer and the right timing because you can end up ruining part of your lifestyle and relationship. I remember when I met my lovely queen, God showed me that she can be the person for my life. Before I knew it, God had me in tears because I thought that Judith was too young for me. But Jesus spoke to my heart and showed me not to look on the outer appearance but look to the heart and I felt such a great peace within me. I held back by talking to her and she came to me without me telling her that God had spoke to me about this, and she said that I was to be her help mate. I was shocked and stunned. Then, I laughed in joy and told her what had happened to me which clarified and confirmed that we were to be together in spite of the age difference. That is faith.

When we were engaged, we wanted to get married right away. But her father and my mother told us well what is the hurry? But her father said to us, why don't you get married in September the 1st? We were at first unsure about this wait, but then the Lord spoke to us and showed us that there is something in timing with God, that really matters. So we waited to wed, and got married Sept 1st 2013 and it was a perfectly timed. God doesn't really look at how much people are put together on the inside or the outside, but if they wait on his timing, he can move mountains on their behalf. I challenge you to wait on God's strength and not your own. He will make a way no matter what circumstances that follow. You will be pulled through.

Let's talk about positive and negative attitudes. In my lifestyle, I have had some negative thoughts in everyday life. I was not perfect. I admit that I came to wrong decisions and messed up but Jesus took my sores away. Having a negative attitude, can be very dangerous. Meaning, thinking the world's view of thoughts. This makes it difficult in their character and reflects on their everyday walk in life. We tend to lash out on the other side which is people, for no reason. Also, because they just wont let go of their hurts in the past that comes to haunt them physically and emotionally. You can't always blame the devil. As it says, "the devil made me do it." Just take a minute and look back at your thoughts. What are you thinking about? Why are you thinking ugly thoughts? I can never amount to anything. I am stupid. I am a failure. No one loves me. You are going to die. All these thoughts are negative thoughts. And this can be turned to happy thoughts. Just give these thoughts to Jesus. Don't you think He can turn them around for your life? I met a friend, he was a nice guy. We don't really talk anymore. I forgive him, and I still love him, as a friend. But he would always come across very negative in his speech. I explained to him I was going to get a big house one day and ministry will grow. But he said, "in your dreams." That did not let me down because if it wasn't for Jesus, being the center of my life I would take his words to heart which could destroy me. So God pulled me away from this person and I stopped going to see him and his family. And prayed for him to have a positive lifestyle because I know he was wronged in some way back in the past. Don't let this negative thoughts eat you alive. Because this can mess you up physically. And that person won't mount to be what God had a perfect destiny for their life.

Let me explain how we can over come fear,insecurity, and forgiveness people day after day basically waltz in these category which places them in hard struggles for their life style many pupil's can't cope with the problem some choose to ignore the circumstances and go on with life as if it didn't happen and the last percentage of the world today try to cope with stress and don't forgive the other party for some silly reason or not telling the truth about their situation but one analogy at a time the first one is fear .

Fear is a deadly to our minds,heart, and character these terms are like cancer, emboli. Let me rephrase this in the book of James new testament chapter one you will read on sin,please go to the scripture if your heart desire's you will find in verse 12 blessed is man who remains steadfast under trial for when he has stood the test he will receive the crown of life, which God has promised to those who love him .

Verse 13 Let no one say when he is tempted. "I am tempted by God." God cannot be tempted with evil and He himself tempts no one, but each person is tempted when he is lured and enticed by his own desires. Then desires when it has conceived gives birth to sin and sin when it is fully grown, brings forth death. We can over come this matter by not allowing your fears and problems get the best of you that's where King Jesus comes into play like chess board we decide to make our first move that would be in your mind to win against the enemy. But when the hard situations occur we begin to dwell on the circumstance and that's when stress begins to take place. But the Father avoids the situation when we call upon His name. Like the board game, He moves us in a way that we can overcome the other opponent. To capture the other man's game piece, which becomes check mate. Getting back to fear, people face a lot of fears. And the fears come from, worrying, and doubt which can lead to sickness in your lifestyle. But when we have King Jesus in our life, we are more than conquerors through Him. People think that fear is natural to have, but not so. If you just take a minute to think like Jesus would think, I challenge you to bring your thoughts your emotions and bad habits to the Father, before you know it if we confess truly to God He will vanish them away for your lifestyle. One day my wife and I were in classes and part of the discussion was on fear not knowing what to do in a tough situation. I raised my hand up as a girl was speaking and she discussed in a negative way so I corrected her in love that God will stand by your side in difficult times by taking away pains anxiety from your emotions which causes fear. Sometimes we face fear of dying but when you have a positive attitude and it is not your time yet, you can overcome and fight with Jesus so that you will not die.

We over come these fear especially sickness to serious illness that is why if you practice your faith in Jesus that is believing for the impossible. I remember a pastor from Toronto he was so weak and tired he could not understand why he losing weight feeling very pale he went to see his doctor and discover he had cancer in most of his parts of his body so he put his faith to action and didn't accept the doctor's examination I was not there but this beautiful man of God shared with me the circumstances after wards . As weeks went on it seems that he started to read scriptures on healing, months down the road he notice his body started to heal until he was completely restored by King Jesus because he didn't allow fear take his own life that is fantastic miracle don't you think .What God can do for him God will do for you just believe for your miracle it will happen.

I want to speak on insecurity there is majority of people who have a lot insecurity that's because of their mind thinking which follows negative outlook on one self. For example, my wife has told me I could talk about her story. My wife was not very confident in who she was, for example, she was always worrying about what she looked like, who she saw in public, and what they were thinking or judging about herself. One day I told her to try thinking positive thoughts instead of the negative lies of the enemy. I knew she was beautiful but if she didn't do anything about her insecurities she wouldn't be able to see this for herself, and eventually it would keep her back from her God-given destiny for her life. I told her to believe in what God said about her, and to keep a list of what positive qualities she has and who God designed her to be. I told her it was her homework and if she did this every day and listened to what God spoke about herself and not what the enemy spoke, she would eventually become that confident woman God created her to be. When you do what God asks of you, whether it be small or big, in the eyes of God it is very important. He showed my wife what confidence really was, and lifted her spirit. It calmed her soul and relaxed her mind from all the worries which ceased. Now she is able to lift her head up high and call herself a mighty woman of God, because she knows that what God says, is more powerful than what anybody else could ever say about her. Believe in yourself, and know that God has created you. You count in the eyes of God.

I challenge you to start forgiving other people so that God can forgive you for your sins. Let us begin. When I was young and foolish I was in an argument with some friends and they did something to hurt my feelings. For weeks on weeks I never contacted them because I was holding bitterness inside my heart which was not good. I might as well have signed papers to the devil and sided with him for unforgiveness. I told my mom about the situation and she corrected me in love telling me that I needed to go back and forgive them. How can the Lord bless you? And I had some doubts as my mother was explaining. Two weeks later I had bumped into another Christian believer in Christ. And we started talking about forgiveness. He had showed me from scriptures no matter what happens or someone did things to me I was to turn the other cheek. I asked him, what did you mean? He said to allow the person to keep talking and saying what they want to say of his own opinion without getting mad and bitter. I had to swallow humble pie. So I went back to the person and apologized and I forgave him. That was very hard but Jesus turned around the whole situation and we became decent friends. It is not always that we hold back our anger in our situations that are ugly. Try to give it to Jesus, and lay it by His side. He will help you overcome the circumstances of forgiveness. Forgiveness means to forgive even though he or she cheated, or robbed, or lied to you. Especially with slander and gossip. We need to forgive that person Christian or non-Christian. There can be good morals that come out of it. But I challenge you to forgive the other party. Maybe you need to take Jesus as your personal savior. Then you will be able to forgive because He loves you unconditionally no matter what happens. Amen

MY STRUGGLE WITH MENTAL HEALTH.

It was the year of 2011 in April when I just had come out of a winter full of revelations and experiencing the presence of God in wonderful ways. I remember waking up one morning and everything seemed like I was under water. I felt like I was under an emotional waterfall and I could not breathe. I knew that I had fallen into a pit of some sort but I didn't know why and I wanted an answer from God why all of a sudden I felt like I was drowning. I had tried out walking on the water with Jesus and it was amazing, so why was I drowning now and I didn't see it coming? I started to experience a lot of panic attacks alone in my home. Nothing would trigger it except that I felt fear and a lot of it. I was living with my Mother and step father and little half sister at the time who was only 5. My mom was busy a lot with her since she demanded attention and I didn't have anyone else to go to so I would drive to the beach and pray every day/ I remember one panic attack I thought my life was ending and I showed up at my counselling center at 8 am in the morning to wait till someone got there to open up. That was the only place I thought I could go to that felt safe. I felt very unprotected and very afraid I was going to die. I didn't know at the time that I was experiencing heavy panic attacks because God was taking me back to a time that was very scary to me as a little girl. I wouldn't know till later that I had waded in a little deeper water just like a little girl would if she only saw her daddy and didn't know there were deep waters ahead of her. My counselor at the time didn't see it coming and no one in my life knew why it was happening.

A lot of people told me that spiritually I needed to wrestle with God and that he would take me through this turbulence as I drew nearer to him. That the enemy was attacking me and I needed to stay close in my prayer closet to Him. My mom, at the same time, and I do love her very much, did what she thought was best at the time for her family by sending me away to my fathers house who I didn't spend much time with. I had a lot of resentment and bitterness from when I was a child and didn't want to stay with him at all. There was no other choice though and as I stayed with him I was triggered right left and centre and the panic attacks increased. I felt like I was a little girl all over again who was very scared of the world and of her earthly father. I remember at night waking up and sensing this very real and deep pull inside from the Holy Spirit calling out for me, yearning for me. I knew that God was very real and was a very jealous lover and very much concerned and watching over me. At the time I felt like I was being chased down by Him, by my Lover. And he was very much a lover of my soul to me. I was afraid but I was very intrigued too. God had shown me through scripture months before and was working on me up till the panic attacks started, that he was very in love with me and loved me as a man would love a woman. I felt so beautiful around the presence of Jesus and felt very very close to His spirit.

THE DARK NIGHT OF THE SOUL

For about two years I went through what some have called the dark night of the soul. It is when something, and in my case, it was anxiety and depression, comes at you and stirs up your soul into a storm. You feel like your whole world is crashing around and you have no ground to stand on. This is where I began to dig my heels in and to face my trust issues with Jesus. I needed to be standing on Him not on my circumstances and environment. I felt like all the people I knew in my life had forsaken me and that meant to me that Jesus forsook me too in my time of need. I had so much going on emotionally and I needed to pour my heart out to God, knowing that he would restore me. I felt like a mess, and I felt like everyone around me could see that I was a big mess. I went through most of this journey on my own, until I met my husband Paul. During this time I chose to trust God whatever that looked like. I would practice His presence which brought peace. I worshiped and praised Him which drove away depression. The more I did this, the more I came out of the dark night of my soul. I would journal my anxieties and pray them out. During this time, I felt like I would never get out of it, I would always remain in this place of darkness and depression where there was no hope. But slowly baby step by baby step,. I got out leaning on my Lord Jesus Christ. I learned this walk with Jesus was not a sprint, it was a walk, of endurance and trust. You didn't need to know where you were going, all you needed to know was the next step and that Jesus was with you in it all. I had no idea how I would get there so I just gave up trying to figure it all out and that's when I started to move forward.

This was one of my favorite verses from Psalms 23: 1-6 and still is today.
The Lord is my Shepard
I shall not want
He makes me lie down in green pastures
He leads me by still waters
Even though I walk through the valley
Of the shadow of Death
I fear no evil
For you are with me
Your rod and your staff comfort me
You prepare a table before the presence of my enemies
You anoint my head with oil, my cup overflows
Surely goodness and mercy shall follow me wherever I go.

My challenge to you would be to trust in the Lord with all your heart, and lean not on your own understanding through the dark night of the soul. Whatever your enemies may be, mine was anxiety and depression, you can overcome them by taking baby steps of faith and trusting in your closest friend, Jesus Christ. When you are in the dark, you cant really see the end everything around you is dark. But when you obey God by praising His name, and prayer to essential things to your walk with God, you will increase in your faith and that brings you through each day. God told me to do those things in the dark, to praise His name. It didn't make sense to me then because I didn't see anything to be thankful for. But He did. He sees the end from the beginning, so praising His name would be like a flash of light getting me out of the dark. I began to praise Him, and I would see my mountain move. It felt so overwhelming sometimes and I felt like the mountain would never move. But praising Him and thanking Him and praying, brought miracles in my life. He didn't take me out right way, but he did give me life light love and grace for the journey. Most of all he stayed very close to me through the journey even when I didn't feel like he did. Most of the people in your life will not understand this part of your journey and you may feel alone, don't give in and don't give up. God kept telling me when I would go to him and complain that this would pass. I had to believe Him and I had to trust Him. I had no one else to get me through this season, and remember, it IS only a season however short or long it may seem. I knew that He was my only way out, so I had to stay close to Him. I had no desire to read the word, no desire to pray, and no desire to worship Him. But I did anyway, because I knew it was the only way. Jesus is the only way. People go through the dark night of the Soul because God is bringing them closer to Him, and these times are the only times you really learn to trust Him. You need Him, and he wants to be that source for you. He wants to develop your faith and this is one of the ways he does that. It's not that you did anything bad, but most times its because you were doing something right, and this happens because God is drawing you into radical trust and radical relationship with the Master, Jesus Christ.

DO NOT BE AFRAID OF THE LIGHT

I learned that to get clean, sometimes you need other people to know your sins. When you are adopted in the family of God, you don't need to be ashamed of the light shining on areas in your life that need to be changed. You need to have the exposed first to even know they are there, and then you can take it out. Religion teaches you to hide or run from your sins, from the light, but Jesus says to come, and let Him wash you and change you. You need to come to the light, and I found it is so much more better when you are surrounded with people who love you and support you every step of the way. In the word it says "come to me all who are weary and heavy burdened and I will give you rest." So many times we don't know how to lay our burdens down and it weighs us down. The light can help you see what burdens you are holding onto and then you can lay them down. If you keep running in the dark because you are afraid of the light, then it defeats the purpose of why Jesus died for you. So that you could be in the light., Don't be afraid of what others will think of you, Jesus sees you as you are and wants to love you and cherish you as you are. When you come into the light, with all the mess and brokenness that comes with you, you can be transformed and enveloped by the Love of God. Usually the ones that judge you are the religious people, the ones who have never experienced the trust and love that comes with knowing an intimate and beautiful God. Only what Jesus thinks truly counts in the end. Jesus says that he came to save the sinners and the sick. He didn't come for those who are already righteous. The sicker you are, the more of the Doctor you will see. He is your Doctor and wants to heal you. All you need to do is approach the light, which is Himself, Jesus Christ, and he will heal you. "I am the way the truth and the Life."- Jesus Christ.

You may ask, how do I lay my burdens down? Burdens are a little different than sins. But as you keep carrying them yourself, it can become sin because you are destroying your temple because you were never meant to carry those things by yourself. They were meant to be pinned to the cross along with your sins. Burdens affect how you see yourself. If you carry so much, its hard to get a good look at yourself, who you were meant to be as a free person of Jesus Christ. You are carrying a lot of extra weight around and baggage. You hold onto so much shame, guilt condemnation worry that you cannot see any more clearly. You need to let it go, put it down and let Jesus come and minister to your weary heart. How? By confessing your sins to Him first, because that opens up the relationship so that he can come and sweep you off your feet. He cannot really go near sin because he is so Holy. He wants to draw near to you though, so confess your sins and draw near the light and he will draw near to you.

"draw near to God and He will draw near to you."

After you confess your sins, linger with Him in His presence, Delight in Him telling your needs and wants. Tell Him whats on your heart, He already knows what is in your heart. Nothing is hidden. He sees everything and desires you to talk to him about everything. As you pour our your heart to Him He will draw closer to you. His presence will flood you as you are more honest to Him, his love will flood you. Ask Him to take care of you, to take your burdens from yourself. You will most likely feel lighter as you tell him your feelings and thoughts. Sometimes it feels like nothing is happening but it is. Other times you feel so much lighter, cleaner and freer. Know that all he wants is to have you draw near to Him through relationship, and fellowship. There is a calmness deep within your spirit and God wants to draw it out. It can sustain you through the roughest seasons of your life. As you nurture yourself by taking the time every day to talk to Jesus, He will reveal this calm, this peace, deep within you. It is the fruit of the spirit, called peace. We need peace to get through the tough times. It sustains us and as we cry out to God and take time to talk he will fill us with everlasting peace. He always wants to draw out your joy that also is a seed that lives inside of you if you are a believer already. As you spend more time with Him, that joy deepens. Its in an everlasting well that lives deep within you.

An everlasting well that lives deep within you....
In the sacred place
where only God and I can roam
Its not in a room, or at the beach
It dwells deep inside
Where hope shall arise
Where God sweeps in
And inside plants a seed
An everlasting well
Of peace that draws you in
Of love that makes you spin
You don't have so much to say
You sit there and linger away
And you know that the One is with you
You're not alone, He dwells in you
You don't have to reach too far
His presence is like the morning star
It starts small inside and grows
As you give seeds to sow
It lasts forever
And draws people together
This light deep within
Of warmth and truth
It overcame sin

Sometimes you weep
Sometimes you have to seek
But He never leaves you
Nor forsakes you
This sacred place
This secret place
Between God and Me.

I challenge you

There are times when we really get challenges from God. Also our inner most being gives us challenges in our every day life style. I can remember just recently my fiancé had told me not to worry about getting any money. This was not a great time since I had been laid-off from my work place and was receiving unemployment services. I decided though that I must go to work for a day and a terrible accident happened with my eye. I suppose that we as followers of Christ must pray before we enter into situations so they will not bring us into a jam. I challenge you to step into faith and seek God for wisdom as the scripture states in james 2:14-20 and Philippians 4:6. There are times we need every day challenges for our lifestyle so Jesus can drive you on the right course which patience comes into play. James 1:3. This is why we ask the holy spirit of truth for guidance towards decisions of making the right choices for our lifestyle of a daily walk with Jesus. I have faced and experienced different styles of living and it did not accomplish very much. Just coming to terms that Jesus is the only way to truth and everlasting life. I challenge you to try Jesus as your lord and savior because He can make a big difference in your life. John 3:3-16

My life as a youngster was challenging in many ways, and if I never had Jesus I wouldn't know where I was today. For example at the age of 30 I remember that I was ready to walk back home at night and looked outside. It was a bad snow storm and the temperature dropped to minus 15. I was staying at my friends house and they asked their mother if I could stay overnight but she said no. So I got a little panicked wondering if I would make it home that evening or freeze like a brown popsicle along the road side. That was challenging! So I got enough faith to head home but started to pray as I was bundling up and ready to go. I started outside talking to myself and it was very windy and cold, so I thanked her for having me over and went on my way leaving with my head down to walk home looking up only the odd time to see where I was going. This walk would have taken around a half an hour to reach my place and by the time I reached home I was very surprised to have gotten home within 10 minutes. God had transported me from one place to another. What a miracle! I challenge you to have a faith where God can reach out to you in times of trouble.

Could you ask yourself how blessed we are as followers of Jesus Christ, not knowing where to turn or how to get in the right standing with Jesus. But even though it takes discipline to be on the right track, remember that we can do all things through Christ Jesus.

One time as I was growing in Christ, I remember that I had a dream. This was unusual to most people and would be very scary too. Picture yourself walking in a huge city where there are bombs flying, and guns fireing, sky-scraper buildings dismantling and citizens are frightened about the war taking place. It was quite the dream as I was walking down a major street, and all I can see in this dream is me carrying a long scroll with the bible by my side and I looked beside me and felt someone was there. All I could sense is like showers of rain falling down right in front of me. As we walked closer to a mother and a child the boy was unconscious because his leg was blown away and the mother was screaming aloud. Two different army men came towards me and one of them had a grenade in his hands as he looked at me and the other person beside me. He dropped the grenade with fear. Same with the other soldier that had a machine gun. I started to raise my hand and the boy's leg started to grow back. This was so unusual. I felt when I woke up that God was showing me the end times. Like the two witnesses in revelation 11:1-23. Praise God!

I challenge you to cast all your cares on Jesus so that He can do a lot of miracles in your lifestyle. Its for the better. Even if you are not saved which you will be in the long run, because I believe after reading this book you will want to know Jesus Christ. At most times we need to focus on the Lord Jesus Christ in our daily walk with Him. I Remember going to a benny hinn crusade. I could remember him speaking a powerful word to the crowd and a miraculous healing went on. As I listened carefully I came to see that people started to interrupt the holyspirit and benny hinn shouted "silence! No one talking right now." When benny hinn expressed by God, I could listen very carefully God telling benny hinn to keep the crowd silent and them talking back and forth with eachother with the holyspirit. The reason for this is that he was showing benny hinn a small task in what he had to do at the service. And that comes with obedience. Have you ever wondered when God speaks to you and you get distracted when he's trying to tell you a beautiful word for some reason we either mess up or don't follow up with what he is asking. Jesus likes to challenge everyone to hear His word and obey in what He tells us for our own good. Can you picture yourself being that obedient? In romans 5:1-8, it talks about the peace and joy for an example, verse 2, explains through whom we have gained access by faith into this grace in which we now stand and we rejoice in hope of the glory of God. Verse 3, not only so but we also rejoice in our suffering because we know suffering produces perseverance, perseverance produces character and character which comes with hope and does not disappoint us because God has poured out His love into our hearts by the holyspirit. I want to speak on prayer, if we as children of the Lord pray without ceasing every day, I find that our walk with Jesus begins to to draw us closer.

Let us look at some scriptures that we can focus on prayer, not as a routine but as a daily lifestyle to increase our walk against the principalities of darkness and also to speak to the great Jehovah. Luke 3:21 explains when all the people were being baptized, Jesus was baptized too. And as he prayed heaven was opened and the holy spirit fell on Jesus like a dove. Another sample psalm 4:1- answer me, when I call to you oh my righteous God. Give me relief from my distress, be merciful to me and hear my prayer. These are some helpful verses to guide us when we pray. Prayer is not just asking God for a bunch of material things or last minute prayer when he or she thinks things are going wrong. I find that people pray to Jesus when they are not following Jesus as their lord and savior especially when they are down or they need something quickly from God and go right back to what they would normally do. Jesus is not a genie where you ask for something and poof its there! First of all when we pray we should always be giving thanks to Jesus Christ in an every day lifestyle which helps to build our character and learn to appreciate in how we can exalt him because when we are able to wake up from our sleep the next day and find out a person you just met yesterday past away that same morning we can feel sorry or we can rejoice in the lord for one circumstance that praise God you are alive and well. Also you can choose to rejoice that this other person went to be with the Lord for eternity. I found when listening to Benny Hinn's teachings in prayer that he acknowledged through Jesus Christ if we have little prayer time we will have less power of the almighty God but if we pray every day without grumbling we can receive more power from Jesus Christ. This opportunity draws us christians closer to encounter Jesus Christ. One day I was sitting on my bed reading the word of God I was younger at the time just reading about the angel visiting Jacob and how God wrestled with Jacob. This intrigued me so I decided to pray for my angel to visit me also. Ten minutes later as I went downstairs to worship and pray, I saw the beam of light come towards me and low and behold the angel started to get closer toward me. I got scared and ran upstairs screaming out to my mother. Next time I should be careful what I pray for.

Prayer could be challenging mentally in your own abilities but when you receive the holy spirit He is able to teach you all things in how to pray. So I challenge you to pray for things hoped for unto God which he knows what is best for your lifestyle. I myself found that if we get anxious and try to do this in our own ability most times the situation can back fire and not work out and that's why we as people should lean on God and not on man. Its like a substance sitting before your eyes and you want it to work out but it does not work out but with God, just believing He brings it together. So if you can have faith in believing for your miracle or situation that is not good or asking favor I challenge you to step outside of the box and trust Him and when you do that its not like the flinstones where a little green marshon snaps his fingers or a genie grants you your wish. It will take some time to receive your favor. Its not always the snap of a finger. God does not work that way. He is a sovereign merciful God who cares for your wellbeing. I want to express my advice for you to trust God for everything. He did it for me and he can do it for you. Have you ever wondered where your life would turn out by yourself and not with Jesus. He makes the big difference in your life. There was a time at the age of 25 when I went to a retreat in colburg Pentecostal camp. I began praying at 10 pm before I went to bed. I was praying to God in wanting different material things. I didn't understand because I was a new born again follower of Jesus Christ so He explained everything to me and as He did I felt very peaceful and that's where he taught me how to pray. As the prayer was finished, I went to bed and had an unusual dream. I dreamt that the sky was lit up and the trumpet blew so loud that every one could hear on the other side of the world and I looked into the sky and saw Jesus and His troops descending from Heaven. I didn't really know what that meant at first and jumped onto the other bed and woke that person up and started crying.

At that moment I really thought the world was ending but this was a dream, and I spoke to a camp counseller and he explained the dream meant that Jesus is coming for His perfect Bride. I didn't know what to say, I was just speechless then he said, Paul you have a very powerful gift, one day God will reveal this to you on this timing not your own. This is why we should wait and believe that God will open the doors no matter what circumstances may occur. Jesus is very understanding. He is not going to zap you out of His will, just believe that He will make a way.

Okay getting back to the benny Hinn crusade, one night while I was there I remember he had a miraculous miracle taking place, it was very powerful. He prayed for people that had heart problems and other situations. I remembered heading back to my parents home that same night and low and behold my mother told me to come upstairs to her room. She had told me some bad news about my uncle, he had a massive heart attack in which he lived in British Columbia. So she had asked me to pray for him and I said well mom I will pray with you in your room for my uncle. She said no that's okay paul go into your room and pray by yourself and I will pray myself. So I told her to have a good sleep and try not to worry about his conditions. God has it under control. As I went into the room I knelt down and started to sing hymns unto the Lord which took place late at night and started to pray hard. I felt a warm feeling come over me and God showed me that everything is going to be okay, that's going into spiritual warfare. Later on that night, I was so exhausted I fell asleep on the floor and picked myself up and rolled into bed. As I was trying to sleep I fell into a deep sleep and the room got ice cold. I couldn't understand. I woke up and low and behold Lucifer was standing by the door staring right at me with a grin on his face, he was so ugly it is hard to describe. A lot of people picture the devil with two horns in his hand but that is not so; He had a long face and was very grey. His jaw bone was at least 6 inches long. And his eyes were sunken into his head. He was very unpleasant to look at. Very dark. I remember I screamed and ran out of the room and was not looking where I was going but just staring at the evil one. In my parents home it is a split level home. Just running out the door there is a stairway and the rail and I ran towards that and out of the blue my younger brother caught me from running off the rail, which would have broken my neck. If it wasn't for Jesus using my brother to catch me I would have been dead. My parents came into the room and my mom rebuked the evilness that was there because the room was so cold. My dad walked in and walked right out. My younger brother phil thought that there was a robber coming through the window to break in. It wasn't so. It had been a tough situation all because I was interceding in prayer for my uncle so he would not die. This gave me such a fright. Now remember, always be ready in season and out of season, pray without ceasing. And don't let the enemy trick you into death. So I went back to sleep and said some prayers and the room became very peaceful with the presence of God roaming inside the room. Praise God what a mighty God we serve! I challenge you to always be tuned with Jesus Christ, even in the tough times because He will make a way for you expecially when you are not serving Him, he will draw you close to him and come back from the world and into His presence. Jus remember He picked you out of billions of people, there is a purpose plan and pursuit for your life. We need to be ruled by the fathers love, 1 cor 13:1-13, its like that song where in the phrase of the song explains, "Open my eyes, search me inside, I can't live without your presence, I can't live without your presence." when I heard that song for the first time, I wept.

SEEKING GOD.

There are times with God when you are mounting on eagles wings, and soaring high above the rest. Then there are the times when you are in the deep valley, and the desert of our souls and you feel unmotivated, dry and weary. God desires us to seek him day and night. He desires us to seek him with all our hearts. He wants a seekers heart because He is The Seeker of our hearts. The most important thing in life I believe is to know God and be known by Him. It is to walk in the cool of the garden with Him before any of the sin began, when it is just you and Him. God desires us to seek him through all seasons, the times we feel wonderful and the times we feel down and dry. The harder times I learned is when you find yourself in the valley, when you really have to press through and be consistent. It is the times when you don't see anything happening or necessarily feel anything taking place but by faith you walk. By faith you apply the word to your life, and by faith you wake up and do your devotions and time with God before anything else. It was very hard for me to adjust to this season because I was so used to the fuzzy feelings of being with God and having him woo me. I was so used to Him showing up every time I called on Him and being able to write in my journal something else God did to amaze me, which was almost every day. I could hear Him clearly, and I walked closely to Him. When I went into what I call the "dry spell" I felt so distant from him. In reality I wasn't because in his word he says "I will never leave you nor forsake you". But this time I had to take the word to my heart and really listen to it because my circumstances and my feelings were not matching up to the word and what the word says about me and my inheritance as a child of God. I was poor financially, materially, and felt poor spiritually too. I had a hard time listening and hearing the voice of God and it was getting me down on myself. I had to put one foot in front of the other every day and walk by faith and not by sight. I had to really ask myself, and see, if the word of God was really my ultimate Authority in my life. I had to believe in the word more than my emotions because my emotions were out of control. I had to trust that the word was enough, that I didn't need to hear his still small voice every day, that I could find Him in the word every day and for that to be enough for me. I felt abandoned and rejected but he wasn't doing that at all, he was actually developing me, and I was getting hungry spiritually working up a good appetite for God. He was developing a seekers heart in me, to seek God with all my heart. It is so easy to seek Him when you get what you want right away, and you see results. But it is when you don't see those results right away, that seeking after God seems harder to do. But as you press through and do it anyway, God will meet you he is just developing in you persistence and character. I was really inspired by some of the leaders we know as Kim walker, who is known as a seeker of God someone who really seeks after His presence, and His heart. And she had to press in one time for months before actually getting a break through. She did what she was to do faithfully every day but one day she got a visitation from Jesus Himself and was changed forever which launched her into her ministry. If we never develop a seekers heart of the Lord, we are missing out on the pursuit and we are missing out on a huge love story between the Lover and you, the loved one. He seeks us, and we in return seek him. It's a love story and it is an honor to seek out the one true God and King of our hearts. God says in His word, if you seek him with all of your heart he will be found by you. He will give you rest and refreshment. Love and words of encouragement. His presence can change you in 2 seconds of being in it with Him, than 3 hours of counselling, or being somewhere else. We become seekers of His presence when we press in and find Him. His presence is that good, that we will want to seek it out once we have experienced it once. At the beginning, I experienced His presence all the time, very easily. When this stopped, I thought something was wrong with me. Instead of seeking him more, I questioned everything about myself, if I was losing my relationship with Him. But he wanted me to seek Him deeper, more, to draw in deep, into the wells of salvation. He wanted me to be built up to be rooted into Him. It takes pressure sometimes, and struggle to get to that desired place with God. Have you ever heard of the butterfly that comes out of His caccoon? If he does not struggle and press through the caccoon, as a caterpillar on his own, he will die and never become that beautiful butterfly. But if he struggles and gets through on his own, he emerges as a beautiful butterfly, no longer tied to the ground, but with beautiful wings that he can fly and soar with. The same is with us spiritually. We sometimes go into a caccoon where God surrounds us, and no one can help us out, we have to press and squirm and there is resistance, to get to that sweet butterfly. If someone comes and helps us out, we may die and never become fully developed. God may be taking people out of your path or you may not find any people around to help you and you may feel rejected. You may not see what is really going on, God may be putting you into a caccoon and you may need to go through this on your own with God, he may be developing you. I challenge you in this time to become a Seeker. That you take this caccoon time as an exciting growing time and not what I thought it was at first, which was a trap and annoyance. Take this time to seek your Lover of your soul, who so much wants to be sought after. Seek Him day and night, and you will find Him. You will find beauty and rest and refreshment. (strengthen me with raisons, refresh me with apples for I am faint with love.- song of songs 2:5) Take this time to grow. Seek the one who has been seeking you since the time you were born. He has spoken to you since you were a baby, till now. He was seeking after your heart. Take the time to seek after His heart. Let yourself be developed, be patient in this time, I know it might hurt and the pressure may be painful. But patience, you are growing! Don't take the easy way out by letting people do the work for you, people may want to help you but let God gently guide you through this process. He will speak to you, and he will meet you. He will meet your brokenness and he will meet your mess, and your struggle. Be patient in seeking Him, and look to the reward. He rewards those who seek Him. The reward is His beautiful presence, to know Him personally deeper than before. He wants to be known. We all want to be known and God has placed that desire in us. Because we are in the image of God, God always wants to be known and sought after. God is very romantic and loves love stories of the lover chasing after the beloved and the beloved turning to the lover. Get caught up in this love story yourself. You may not feel so loved, or a part of something so beautiful, but it is real. Trust me, His love is like a fire that burns and nothing can quench it. His presence is like that fire, wouldn't you want to be inside that fire that is never quenched? (for love is as strong as death, its jealousy unyielding as the grave. It burns like a blazing fire like a mighty flame. Many waters cannot quench love, rivers cannot wash it away. Song of Songs 8:6-7) It is worth pursuing. And when the pain of that shell breaks you, he will be there to carry you even further. This place of seeking, and being sought by God is a very intimate time. It might not seem like it, but he is working. He is drawing you closer to Him. It takes time but to have a seekers heart is his desire for us, to chase after Him. For all of eternity we will be getting to know our lover. Why not start now?

Seeking God can look like a lot of things. If you are creative, you can seek him through dance, through the arts through poetry. If you love nature, you can seek him through walks, looking at the stars going to a beach. Reading the word is important to do every day because the word is His very life, and it cleanses us and refreshes us. It corrects us and guides us. It is his very light that we need each day. Singing songs and worshiping him are ways to seek his face. Talking to him or journaling to him are also ways to seek Him. There are so many ways to seek His heart, sometimes its just being silent and letting him heal you. Every time you seek him, he sees. He knows everything and nothing goes unnoticed. You will be rewarded, just don't ever give up. He will come, just like the dawn . "For I am the Lord your God, who takes hold of your right hand, and says to you, do not fear, I will help you."-Isaiah 41:13

The Fathers love and Faith like a Child

One day I was laying in my bed just soaking in the Lord's music. Soaking is to just lay there and allow the music to bring you closer to Jesus. As I was laying there, so desperate to know Him, I was shown a picture from the Lord In my heart and mind. It was a picture of a little two year old girls feet. Jesus was washing her feet between her little toes. I knew immediately as it flashed before me, that this little girl was me and those were my little feet. My eyes were on the Lord and he took me to a place of deep worship where he showed me the fathers love for me. He loves me and wanted to demonstrate that love by just being with me to wash my feet. I had been through a lot of suffering at the time and was going through a trial and really needed to see the love of the Father for me. How I was just a little girl in the eyes of a big father and he was just washing my feet, delighting in my little feet, who He created for Himself. He was tenderly washing me, and soaking me in this water. I needed to see this to know how the Father wants to be with me. He delights in his creation and wants us to be just as deeply delighted in Him as our father. Demonstrating the love of God is deeply communicated through out worship. Laying down ones life for another is a place of deep intimacy God wants to take us to as our Father. If anyone has not been through a good relationship with their father, know that you can experience the Fathers love through Jesus Christ. He demonstrated His love for us when he died apon the Cross and became like us so that he would bring us back to the Father, who delights in us. He loves us so much and doesn't see us the way we see ourselves. In fact, he wants us to climb apon His lap so that we can be told who we are by spending time with Him. He brings us up higher when we come to him and lay down all our concerns and give Him our time and our love. Enjoyment and pleasure is one of the greatest things the Lord, our Father created. He created this so that He could enjoy and find pleasure in the ones He created and so that they could come to find pleasure and enjoyment in the Father. So many times I have seen people who are worn out on religion and weary from the battles they've faced. They come to the Father and just collapse in his arms too tired to carry themselves anymore. And that was not the way God created us to function. He wants us to have a soundmind, and peace, but instead we are weighed down by anxious thoughts, weary burdens, and we forget even why we were created. So many people I have seen have sold themselves to others, in an attempt for temporary security and a sense of identity, but I have learned that nobody owns me. There is only One who owns me, and that is Jesus Christ and God the Father and the Holy Spirit. He desires to know me. He is the only one who deserves of my life, because he paid the price for that life. To forget that and go on with my life, is like forgetting that the one who really died for me, is not a part of my life because of my choice to reject him. God will not make you choose him, he wants you to choose him out of love, not out of control. You can trust Him to own your life when he paid such a big price for it. He died, his blood poured out, naked and nailed to the cross for all to see. He paid a huge price, so he would never treat you poorly, and never lead you astray. You can know that he has the best interest for you. He would only take really good care of you and be a great friend to you if you would just let him in to your heart and life.

Being a child of God is really quite easy. Its not a job, its not wordly understanding. Being a child of God has to be revealed by the Holy spirit to you, and you would know you are a child of God because He would reveal it to your heart. Being a child of God means you get to climb apon the lap of the creator of the universe and he will tell you secrets to your heart, and you would be free in His presence. He brings you closer to your heart through being with Him. Its not a striving thing. One of the things I had to learn the hard way and I believe can be a learning curve for a lot of christians and it takes faith to get to this place, and sometimes a lot of trial and error, is that we feel deep deep down in our core that we are not good enough, or worthy enough for Jesus. So we strive and strive and strive to earn His grace, his unmerited favor, his love and acceptance of us. So much that we grow tired and faint, and we most likely turn back or give up. But God is calling us into a new place. He is saying much more these days to his beautiful Bride. He is calling us home, to a higher place than we have ever been or seen or imagined. He has planned before creation of this intimacy of love, and of grace, this quiet place of understanding between Him and His creation. Its yearning, even the creation itself, is yearning for this quiet place. To be redeemed back to the place and time when God created Eden and adam for Himself. It was a quiet trusting inimate place, that only God and Adam could be. Eventually Eve came in and there was an even deeper intimacy between the three of them. But it was a place of no striving. It was a place of deep deep rest, deeper than we have even understood. But Adam was afraid of how he was made and so was Eve, and they broke communion with God. They didn't understand what it was, but they were naked and ashamed and ran from their Father. He loved them so much that he even clothed them after they deliberately disobeyed them in the garden of eden when they ate that apple. God knew that someday, He would bring them back to this place of deep intimacy through his Son, the Perfect One, the Perfect Atonement, and that at this age in time, He would recreate this reaction between the Father and the people and would bring them back to the Father who knows them.

But I hear the Lord telling me to tell this to His people: My people don't know why I died for them. They have heard all the wrong answers from man. My people need to know that I don't need them. I want them, but I don't need them. When I created them, it was out of my passion and out of my goodness, that I just wanted to bless my heart. I am a worshiper at Heart and I wanted to give out of the abundance of my heart. I bless. Its what a Father does. And I give Life, that's what I am about. I am a God of love, and not control that's why I don't convert people to me, instead of that, I am a God who woos them to me. I am about connectedness. A lot of people have been misunderstood about who I am and why I came. I died so that people who didn't know me who wanted to know me would see me. I died so that I could be One with you again. I wanted to bless you so I made you. I didn't have to but I wanted to because I believed in you as my beautiful creation. You have my seed in you. When I made you I had a plan. A beautiful plan. But I must get this message across, I made man for myself. I didn't make you for someone else. Noone else can create you like I did. No one can tell you who you are.

But before I go on, i want to share something about the Father. His heart is close to children. He loves the little children of the world. And he says let the little children come to me for theirs is the kingdom of Heavan. He delights in us as little children. And He looks at us with joy because to him we are his children, who don't know a lot yet but are learning as He guides us hand in hand. So we don't need to beat ourselves up, or tear ourselves down when ever we mess up. He wants us to love ourselves the way he loves us. He wants us to take pride in who we are because our Father created us. And unless we come as little children to Jesus, we will never be able to enter the kingdom. He wants to laugh with us and let go with us, let that burden go that negativity that the world can rub off on you and renew your youth in His presence. He birthed us and he desires us to go through life with Him, come to him for everything, and bring everything to him. He deeply hurts for us when we are hurt, and he deeply cares for us like no one could ever care. So hang on, anyone who is in deep waters right now, because God the Father wants to share with you His mercy and love. He wants to assure you its not the end of the world. Sometimes things are tough but when you just rest in the rest of God, you learn that its just a season and that you are being guided by Love. By Jesus Himself. He never lets you go. And he never lets you die. He never gives up on you, even when you give up on yourself. So hang on.

Believing in Jesus is a child like thing. You have to just trust that He is there, hanging on to your hand and that you are safe in his arms. If you don't have this child like faith yet, let it enter you. You can't go wrong. You have nothing to loose, but to empty yourself on Him and He will take you as you are. It might not feel nice at the time, but He knows you. You have to trust Him that He can wipe your tears away and bring you out of that pit. He can do anything if you believe like a child would believe in her Daddy or his Daddy. He never said you have to be perfect to be in His grace. All you have to do is be. He designed you to be. Come as you are and he will show you the love you have always been aching for. He knows what you need and he knows you need to be loved and held. This world can get rough, like rough tides crashing on the shores, but He is calling us home. He says "take up your cross my beloved and come to me. I know you by name and you are mine. In time, you will forgive yourself, you will believe again, you will have a new heart." You don't have to try with God.

Jesus wants us to know His Father. He has a new name for you. He has a new home for you, and He will lead you there step by step. He will show you the Father and He will show you who you are to Him. Come to Him, yield your heart to him and you will find his mercies and the truth. You were created by him, for him. As you yield your life to Him, he will show you amazing things, and do amazing things in your life. Don't try too hard, all it takes is a little faith the size of a mustard seed and courage, boldness to come to the throne of grace and he will, Jesus will meet you there. When you come, come in expectance that the Father, who created you and designed you in His image, did not forget about you, and was waiting for you, for this time to come for you to come to Him and acknowledge him. The rivers will open up and heaven will reign down on you. He died for you, believe it in your heart and he will start to do a new thing in your life. He wont ever let you go. He is not a man that he should lie. Believe it for you are never going to be let down by your Father. I hear Him wooing our hearts right now to him, with a love too deep for words. Longing for that place of intimacy to return to Him and His bride. He is here, and he is calling us to come to him just as we are. To simply place our trust in him. Some of you have broken pasts, and mistrusted others, and are in bitterness and unforgiveness but the Lord wants to take that all away from you. If you will take that first step of faith to come back to that place of trust and love with Jesus, he will take away all your past pains and hurts and make you new. He created you and can and will recreate you. You are beautiful. And a child of God.

THE FATHER'S LOVE

I hope that this book spoke in your life. It's not always that Christians or believers in Christ Jesus honor the lord with all our hearts. we should honor our lord in everything first before making any decisions so many people end up making the wrong choices in their life styles and attend to blame God for their own conduct but that is not so. Believers and non-believers both like doing things their own way until they get hurt. So if you take 30 seconds or just wait and believe that God can use anyone even a donkey to speak into your life this opportunity will make your choices with lots of wisdom instead of being unsure about one self . In the book of James 1:6-8 talks about the person who doubts like a wave of the sea,driven and tossed by the wind ; which makes a double minded person .I believe if you make the right decisions you can be better off than you were before that builds up your personal character. So any person will not have low self-esteem about one self, but I encourage you to think positive about yourself which makes you feel better in all your ways. Getting back to honoring God. I made some silly mistakes over the years but just putting Jesus first in my life made me very positive and having a good attitude in everyday life this method comes with faith,worship,praying and meditating on the word of God .Honoring God is not a chore but it is friendship also having that pure understanding love of God for he can be your poppa as you allow Him to work in your lifestyle. You can become a different person as you watch what he can do, please trust in him.

Imagine the terrible things that happen in your life style especially hurts, bitterness and resentment but a lot people just don't know how to deal with these issue's so part of the population pretend without showing their emotions try to deal with this, others just don't think about the situation and low and behold depression begins,fear takes place,and confusion starts within your mind . Gods love can break all these negative mind settings,just to let you know he cares deeply and loves you unconditionally without batting an eyelash. My Queen and I experienced this situation in our lives and with the help of Jesus Christ, we both came out on top. This was not an overnight quick fix deal this process can be healed depending on your faith and how much brokenness he or she has. The key is a lot of patience, patience with the process of healing and patience with yourself.

Eventually as time flies he or she can be restored by Jesus' unfailing love, having that faith to believe. 1Corinthians chapter 13:13 which refers to the love chapter from the bible and other people can have very deep hurts,and pain which over powering their life style can hinder their walk with God and leave them more subject and vulnerable to the demonic realm in which Satan then has a foothold.

The enemy is very cunning and very deceitful, advocate will twist words right around to make you believe that you're doing right thing in you're mind and heart, Allow me to explain how Lucifer came about for any one who does not know about this . At the time of the creation, there was Arch angel who was named the bright and morning star as when Great Jehovah God placed giftings such as music for he was in charge of praise and worship and all the other angels but because of pride,jealousey and wanted to take over Gods position. From my understanding there was no honor to my poppa, according to the cannon which we call the bible you will find that God and Lucifer is mentioned in the scriptures of the old testament in the midst of all this Lucifer was cast out of the first heaven with his one third of his Angels .I hope this information will allow to open your heart and to understand his love, and mercies for your life . Let me refrace this jesus paid the price for our sinful ways so we can have everlasting life with the father forever plus He loves you so much it doesn't matter what circumstances you had faced today tomorrow,and past because Jesus has never changed he's the same today, yesterday, tomorrow check it ! Jeremiah 29: 11 which explains that God knows the plans for your well being,not to harm you but to restore you completely from any wrong turns, He planned and made a beautiful destiny for each and every one .Lay your troubles before King Jesus he waiting at the door for you so don't be held by the prisoner of fear. Jesus can brighten up your day even in the bad days and have a positive attitude about your self don't let anyone tell you that you are ugly because you are beautiful regardless or stupid,low selfesteem,can't amount to anything all these accusations are false lies from Lucifer that' not love .

God's love is perfect it endures peace,joy, laughter, kindness,not seeking glory for one self,but having faith to believe in the now .

When you are feeling down lonely or upset have you ever made any decision or questioned yourself?

We can over come the mix feelings by denouncing your troubles to Jesus, don't forget he is the author and finisher of circumstances that follows you in our every day life, if we don't deal with the issues this can overcome your way of thinking than pride sets itself in the mind . So just ask Jesus to take these burden away the process may take a while depending on deliverance with your pastor or spiritual healing clinic after that is done you can celebrate the victory in Jesus as an testimony of your faith healing.

God love endures forever he care for you and I he is very passionate merciful, full of grace, he set high standards for your destiny to give you the first best he understand how you feel, he there to be your true friend he will never leave you or forsake you, he wants to break away the tough challenges we face in life. He knows you by your name, and calls you out to follow Him. You can breathe when you are with Him because He loves you. You can relax with Him and let go in His love. When we are with the Father, we don't have to be afraid. He takes all our fears away because He holds us and whispers to us His love. He makes us laugh, and He is with us when we cry. We can always climb up onto his lap, whether we have been good or bad, because we are wrapped in His grace, and He never sends us away. He loves when we are in His lap, and would never tell us we are bad. We are all learning, so we are all accepted, no matter of what level we are at. So I challenge you to acknowledge the fathers love for your life only he can turn you around just give him a try he is waiting for you and see the beautiful exploration of an agape love he has in store for us.

love of our heavenly father is so unique he forgives any sin that we may endure with this life style and wants us to come in open arms to him .In 1John 5:3 explains through his love we are to obey his commandments and his commandment are not a burdensome. So we can endure his faith to believe for the impossible circumstances. Amen!

God created marriage for Himself

When God created Adam in Genisis, God declared that adam needed a help mate and that it was not good for man to be alone. So God created Eve and together they reigned in the garden of eden over all the animals and creatures of the air and fish of the sea. All that God created was good. And He set them apart for Himself in the garden of Eden. They walked in the cool of the day together with God. He had set them aside for His pleasure. However, the serpent, the craftiest creature decided to tempt Eve and got her and in the end adam, to go against what God had told them. They were then banned from the garden and from the presence of God. Because of their ways, God could not allow them to reign with Him anymore. He did however, keep them together. He did not banish eachother from one another. What he created was for good and to enjoy. He still loved adam and eve very much and they were the apple of His eye. Because God is good, he did not tear them apart. He brought them out of eden together, and they stayed together until their time on earth was up. But all over the world, people were adding to the numbers and increasing in their stature and in wealth. What God created was meant for His purposes and His purposes only. What God brings together no one can separate. He meants what He says, whether we break our vows and promises to Him or not. He is still good to us, and even when we don't deserve it. He still keeps His word and does not destroy what is good. So in Genisis it shows us that marriage was created by God and intended for Gods purposes and was in the category as good, therefore it remained after the fall of adam and eve and did not fall apart. They went through the worst kind of situation where they both were tempted and betrayed God and were both sent away in exile, but their relationship lasted, it did not waver. They did not let the liar, the accuser, ruin their marriage what God had brought together. We can all learn from adam and eve. Most people just look at what went wrong but they did something right too. They let God be God, be the centre in their relationship with eachother. They did not let the bad things in life ruin the good. Because God is good, goodness always points to God, because every good and perfect gift comes from the Father of lights. James 1:17.

And goodness is a fruit of the spirit and is an everlasting fruit that remains. Galations 5:22-23. What ever is good has to remain. It cannot be hindered, it cannot be destroyed because it remains forever with God in heaven. It is a fruit of the spirit. God has not destroyed anything that is good from the beginning of time. He made adam and eve and it was good. Gen 1:31. He only destroyed what had become evil in His eyes. But what he made was good and goodness is for eternity and cannot die. He wanted to bring the joy of the Lord to the earth so he created man and woman to bear this joy. He made vessels of earth and brought life to them to bring joy to all the creatures of the earth. Mostly, to God. He wanted to show the world what love was like, so he made a woman for a man. He made them one flesh. Mark 10:8. What He created was not for anyone to take. He made it for himself. God did not design one man for another, he created man for one flesh, for one woman who he has seen before the world began. God does not put one woman on the shelf for one man, just to take that man who he had planned for the one on the shelf to all of a sudden change the chorus of the destiny of this man to another. Because marriage is so sacred, so is the person who is meant for the other person. No other can come in and take away what one promise is for another. In other words, God does not create a man for any girl there is out there. He created you with another being in mind. He does not condemn the person who does not stay with the person they were created for, however, Gods intention from the beginning was for marriage to last forever with just one person you were designed uniquely for. That is why divorce is not looked at very kindly by people because marriage was designed to be forever. However, it does not mean to beat yourself up or condemn the one who has been through divorce. God is not worried about your yesterdays as long as you are turning towards him in a sincere heart, and want to bring all your heart to him. He will take care of every hurt and burden that you have experienced in your life. Sometimes life circumstances are out of our control and we don't know what to do at the time. So we make mistakes based on what we know. God though, in his goodness can cover our mistakes and past but we must acknowledge that we need a Savior and then decide to come to Him and turn from our old ways and lifestyle. There is no condemnation for those who are in Christ Jesus. My friends, you are not condemned if you have been in a divorce. God's heart actually breaks for those who have dealt with this situation before because it is such a heartbreaking situation to go through. He does not want you to deal with this alone. Come to Him when you are struggling or grieving with this, and he will make you whole. Isaiah 53. He wants you to feel no burdens with him, no guilt, no heart break, he wants to heal those who are brokenhearted and cover their sins with his grace. There is a way for you. You are not stuck in a pit that you cannot get out of. God will make a way. He will come to you, just call out to Him and wait apon Him to come and do a great change in you. He will do this for you if you ask Him. He just wants intimacy with you and for you to learn to rely on and come to him for everything. He wants to pick you up again and go forward in life with you. He does not mean for you to be stuck in your ways, because He died for you to get you out of those ways, which only leads to death and accusation. But when you trust Jesus as your Savior, he will make doors open for you and the light will shine on you again.

When we are created for someone, we know we can rest in God's embrace as we wait for them to come to us. We don't need to search around for that person, or wonder and worry if we are ever going to find them. We used to do this when we did not know this but now what are we doing, still searching as if we have no Savior? We are not alone, and we need to know that there is a reason we are here and it has to do with the other person who is also waiting for you. When we begin to trust this, things in our lives begin to change. We don't have to worry as much, we don't have to look as much, or run to this relationship and that one, we begin to let God do all that. We start to bring all our worries to God and we begin to pray and wait patiently for that person that God has specifically for us. We have a plan from God for our lives, each and everyone of us and we don't have to worry about anything that comes in our paths. We are well taken care of by God. He still holds us. We are not cast out, or driven far away because Jesus came 2000 years ago and brought us back into the very presence of God where he drives our worries away. We must not wait a lifetime to get it right when God is literally only a breath away right now. We don't have to have someone else go into the presence of God for us, we can do it on our own right now. We can ask God to make our lives new. If we have gone through a divorce, we had no idea how to deal with it, well God can make it a better situation if you come to Him. We may have to go through a season of dealing with some things that are not perfect, or pleasant, but God will create a new life for you if you stick with it in the hard times and give Him the glory. We are not to expect everything to come to us right away. But we know that if we wait apon Him and trust Him, we will come through and there is a light at the end of the tunnel for us. We must call apon him though and ask him to come into our lives to change us. He alone can help us, no man, no other source can do this for us. We have been there and done that. Now it's time to cry out to the One who knows us, and created us, and the only One who can do this for us, who can make all things right in time. We must entrust ourselves to Him while we wait. Come to Him right now, as we are reading this, and tell him how you feel about your life. Whether or not you have gone through a divorce, it may be something else, a longing and yearning for that person to come into your life, if you are single and waiting. Well, you are reading this for a reason. We are not alone. We are loved by Jesus the Savior of the world. He died for you to be free of all the mess you are in. He didn't come to leave you there in your life the way it is. He is calling you forward out of your mess. He means business. He will conquer whatever you are going through, with you, and bring you out so that you can go and tell the world of what he has done. He will never let go. Come; let's turn to Him now together. Do you want to trust Jesus with your life? Will you turn your sins over to him for a new way of living? It won't come right away but he will do what he says when we call to him.

SALVATION PRAYER

Dear Jesus, I am in a mess in my life and I can't seem to get out of it. God, I don't know you yet, but I hear that you are a good God. That you never meant for me to go through what I went through. I did not know then what I do now. For you know the plans you have for me, not to harm me but to prosper me, plans for a hope and a future. I trust you now with my hope and my future. I bring my plans and my hope to you and ask that you would come and live in me, and reign in me in my life. Please come to me and wash away all my sin and guilt, and give me a new name and a new heart and a new life. Thank you for dying for me on the cross so that I could come into your presence so that I could be with you forever. I pray this in Jesus Name.

There. You have just done the most important thing you could ever do for yourself. You just turned from darkness and have been brought into the kingdom of light! God has begun a good work in you and will finish it. He promises you that. 1Chronicles 28:20. You can begin to laugh again and hope again in your future because you now have a God who will be with you all the way. He will give you the right way to go and He will lead you. He will teach you all things and you will never have to be alone again.

Go in peace and faith. God bless you.

Printed in the United States
By Bookmasters